Original title:
The Snowbound Soul

Copyright © 2024 Swan Charm
All rights reserved.

Author: Daisy Dewi
ISBN HARDBACK: 978-9908-1-1834-5
ISBN PAPERBACK: 978-9908-1-1835-2
ISBN EBOOK: 978-9908-1-1836-9

Reflections in the Icy Silence

In the glow of candlelight, joy is found,
Laughter dances softly, round and round.
Snowflakes whisper secrets, pure and bright,
While the hearts of friends are warm tonight.

Overhead the stars in twinkling glee,
Join the chorus of the winter's spree.
Each moment sparkles like the frost,
In this festive time, we count the cost.

Gifts wrapped with ribbons, colors galore,
Echoes of the past, knocking at the door.
With every carol sung, spirits rise,
Reflecting in the icy, starry skies.

Together we gather, united we stand,
Sharing the joy, hand in hand.
In the heart of winter's serene embrace,
Love shines brightest, in this hallowed place.

The Chill of Remembrance

In twinkling lights, the memories spark,
Laughter echoes in the snowy dark.
Fires crackle, warmth we share,
Hearts aglow, love fills the air.

Candles dance in the winter's breeze,
Whispers of joy riding the trees.
Stories told by the hearth's embrace,
In festive moments, we find our place.

A Breath of Ice on the Windowpane

Frosty patterns weave tales of cheer,
As families gather, the warmth draws near.
Joyful voices rise like a song,
In this season, we all belong.

Snowflakes kiss the ground with grace,
Laughter glints on every face.
Together we share in the glow,
A breath of ice, but hearts all aglow.

Solitary Footprints in the Snow

In a blanket of white, a story unfolds,
Solitary footprints, each one bold.
Glimmers of hope in a frosty land,
Every step taken, hand in hand.

The chill of winter, a dance so bright,
With every twirl, we chase the light.
Festive spirits rise, pure and true,
In snowy meadows, joy breaks through.

Frozen Whispers of Longing

Under starry blankets, we whisper dreams,
Frozen wishes flow like silver streams.
In the quiet night, hearts softly sigh,
As tales of yore drift like snowflakes by.

Each moment sparkles, a gem in time,
Resounding laughter, sweet as a rhyme.
In winter's grasp, love's warm embrace,
Frozen whispers ignite the space.

Frosted Euphony of the Mind

Joyous laughter fills the air,
Colors twinkle everywhere.
Candles glow with warm delight,
A tapestry of purest light.

Families gather, hearts entwined,
With dreams and hope in every mind.
Songs of cheer in harmony,
Echo through the shimmering tree.

Gifts exchanged with tender care,
Voices lift, for love we share.
Moments freeze, like snow so white,
Creating warmth in winter's night.

The Lament of the Winter Spirit

Silent whispers in the frost,
Memories linger, never lost.
Chill winds weave their gentle song,
In the night, where dreams belong.

Yet hope remains beneath the cold,
Stories waiting to be told.
Winter's heart may seem forlorn,
But joy can be reborn every morn.

Underneath the blanket clear,
Magic glimmers, oh so near.
Let laughter break the icy veil,
As spirits dance, they shall prevail.

Ethereal Dance of Snowflakes

Softly falling from above,
Each flake spins like a dove.
In the moonlight, pure and bright,
A whimsical and wondrous sight.

Children's laughter fills the street,
Snowball fights, oh what a treat!
Warmth of cocoa in our hands,
By the fire, together we stand.

As the world turns white and still,
Moments linger, hearts will fill.
Dance of flurries, light as air,
Every twirl dispels despair.

Soul's Winter Journey

In the stillness of the night,
Stars above, a shimmering sight.
Footsteps crunch on fresh, white snow,
Guided by the soft moon's glow.

Wandering through the winter's grace,
Finding warmth in every place.
Hearts unite, with stories shared,
In every glance, affection bared.

Through the chill, our spirits rise,
Together under snowy skies.
The journey's joy is ours to find,
A festive bond, in heart and mind.

Shivering Shadows in the Frost

The twinkling lights dance bright,
As laughter echoes through the night.
With cocoa warm and sweet delight,
We gather close, all hearts in flight.

Snowflakes swirl like wishes spun,
A silent joy, the night begun.
In every heart, a spark, a run,
Together we shine, all as one.

The chill may bite, but smiles stay bold,
With stories shared, each moment gold.
In festive cheer, let's break the cold,
Embracing warmth as joy unfolds.

As shadows flicker, dreams take wing,
In frosty air, our voices sing.
With every hug, we feel the spring,
In shivering shadows, our hearts cling.

Whispers of Cold in the Heart

Crackling fires warm the air,
While outside whispers chill with care.
Yet in this space, we laugh and share,
The warmth within, a bond so rare.

Around the table, tales are spun,
Of frosty nights and winter fun.
We hold each other, one by one,
In every smile, new joy begun.

The world may freeze, but here we stand,
With open hearts, we join the band.
In chilly depths, we take a hand,
And celebrate life, truly grand.

So raise a cup, let spirits soar,
In whispers cold, we seek for more.
Beneath the frost, our hearts explore,
With each embrace, we love and adore.

Beneath the Chill of Isolation

In frosty air, a silent night,
Where shadows linger, dimmed from light.
Yet hope ignites, a spark so bright,
Together we rise, in shared delight.

Through winter's grasp, we journey on,
With every step, the strength is drawn.
Though distance stings, we'll not be gone,
In unity's warmth, a brighter dawn.

The chill may whisper tales of dread,
Yet in our hearts, a fire is fed.
With every laugh, a thread is spread,
Woven in love, where joys are bred.

So let the frost weave silver lace,
In every moment, we find grace.
Beneath the chill, we'll share this space,
Together we thrive, in joy's embrace.

Quietude Wrapped in White

A blanket soft, the earth asleep,
In silence, snowflakes gently creep.
With hushed intent, our secrets keep,
In quietude, our dreams run deep.

The world transforms, a canvas pure,
Where whispers of peace do reassure.
In this stillness, we feel secure,
As laughter and love begin to stir.

With every breath, the crisp air sings,
Of festive joy and simple things.
Wrapped in white, the heart takes wings,
As hope and magic softly rings.

So raise your voice; let spirits shine,
In frozen realms where hearts entwine.
In quietude, our lives combine,
In celebration, let us dine.

Glacial Reflections of the Heart

Amidst the frost, our laughter sways,
As stars above begin to blaze.
With every twinkling, joy ignites,
In winter's glow, our spirit lights.

Soft whispers dance on icy air,
We gather close, without a care.
The warmth of friendship, ever near,
In frosted dreams, we shed all fear.

A tapestry of night unfolds,
In silver hues, a tale retold.
The glacial sheen, a heart so bright,
Reflects the love that feels just right.

Together we will always stand,
In this vast and enchanted land.
With every heartbeat, we will show,
The magic of love in purest flow.

The Solstice of Stillness

As shadows stretch and daylight fades,
In quiet cloaks, the world parades.
A hush descends, so calm, so dear,
In this still night, we find our cheer.

The trees adorned with diamond dust,
In nature's dance, we place our trust.
With flickering flames, our hearts unite,
A cadence soft, a winter's night.

Each breath we take, a whisper sweet,
Under the stars, we find our beat.
The frosty air brings laughter's song,
In this solstice, we all belong.

A gathering of souls so bright,
In warmth beside the glowing light.
This moment shared, forever holds,
The magic of the heart's pure gold.

Waking in a Snow-laden World

Awakened by the softest sound,
A gentle hush blankets the ground.
Eyes wide with wonder, spirits soar,
In this snow-laden world, we explore.

Flurries twirl like dancers free,
Each flake a note in harmony.
With every step, the laughter rings,
In frosty realms, our joy takes wing.

The sun peeks through, a golden ray,
Chasing the shadows of yesterday.
In sparkling white, our dreams take flight,
Boundless and bright, hearts feel so right.

With rosy cheeks, we weave our play,
In this wonderland, we'll stay.
Together wrapped in joy and cheer,
In a snow-laden world, we revere.

Frosted Footprints of Longing

In the quiet, where whispers play,
Footsteps trace the dreams of yesterday.
Each frosted print, a tale unspun,
Of hearts entwined, of love begun.

Through frozen paths where hopes reside,
With every breath, our souls collide.
In winter's hush, a secret shared,
A longing felt, a heart laid bare.

The twilight glows with hints of gold,
In this journey, we, brave and bold.
With every shimmer, we revive,
The frosted footprints, love's alive.

We'll wander through this cherished night,
In dreams and laughter, pure delight.
The path we trace, forever strong,
In frosted footprints, where we belong.

The Cold Embrace of Memory

In the glow of flickering lights,
Old stories dance in evening's hush.
Laughter echoes through the night,
With every heart, a gentle rush.

Snowflakes swirl in dazzling flight,
Each a note in winter's song.
Memories twinkle, pure delight,
As time embraces, soft and strong.

Footprints trace a path of cheer,
Glimmers of joy on frosty ground.
In the warmth, we feel you near,
In every hug, sweet love is found.

With every toast, the past ignites,
In festive cheer, our spirits bloom.
Through the cold, our hearts unite,
Finding comfort in the room.

Frosty Murmurs of Longing

Cold winds whisper through the trees,
Swaying branches, soft and sweet.
Hearts conspire with winter's breeze,
As fog blankets the quiet street.

Frosted windows frame the glow,
Inside, we share our dreams of light.
Every laugh a gentle blow,
Against the chill of the night.

Stars above like diamonds shine,
Each one holding tales of yore.
With a wish upon the vine,
We long for more than just folklore.

In the silence, hopes take flight,
Wrapped in warmth, hand in hand.
In frosty air, love feels right,
Together, we'll forever stand.

Fragments of Warmth in a Frozen World

In winter's grasp, a fire glows,
Where shadows dance and spirits play.
Beneath the sky, where cold wind blows,
We gather here, come what may.

With mugs of cheer, we lift a toast,
To moments shared, and bonds we cherish.
In this embrace, we feel the most,
As frozen fears begin to perish.

Snowflakes fall like confetti bright,
Each one unique, a wondrous sight.
In every flurry, joy takes flight,
Coloring the world in pure delight.

Through frosty nights, our laughter rings,
Echoing warmth as daylight fades.
In every heart, the crisp air sings,
Uniting us in winter's shades.

Dreams Entombed in Ice

Beneath the frost, old dreams reside,
Entombed in layers of still delight.
Yet hearts like flames refuse to hide,
They spark and flicker in the night.

Each frozen breath, a wish sent high,
In every whisper, hope persists.
Through frigid air, we let love fly,
Mending hearts with gentle twists.

Candles flicker, shadows play,
As stories weave a joyful thread.
In winter's chill, we find our way,
In every tear, the warmth is spread.

With every heartbeat, let us rise,
Through ice and snow, our spirits soar.
In dreams entombed, the fire lies,
Awaiting spring to bloom once more.

An Echo Beneath the Snowdrifts

Beneath the glow of twinkling lights,
The laughter dances through the nights.
Snowflakes whisper, soft and bright,
Creating joys in sheer delight.

Footprints mark the snowy ground,
In every heart, the love is found.
Hot cocoa swirls in steaming mugs,
Wrapped in warmth, like tender hugs.

The carols sung, the spirits high,
Underneath the starry sky.
With every cheer, a tale unfolds,
In glowing warmth, the memory holds.

Together weaving dreams anew,
In festive nights of red and blue.
An echo rings, a joyful sound,
In winter's heart, our hopes abound.

Hearts Adrift in Winter's Grip

Frosty windows, glimmering bright,
Gathered close, the warmth ignites.
With every flame, the shadows sway,
In this cozy nook, we play.

Snowflakes spin like dancers fair,
Joyful moments fill the air.
With every grin and every cheer,
We celebrate the winter's dear.

Hearts adrift, like stars above,
Floating gently on the love.
In laughter's echo, secrets blend,
Each story shared, we recommend.

Winter's grip, yet we are free,
Bound together, you and me.
In this season, bright and vast,
We hold the joy, forever cast.

Beneath the Blanket of Silence

Silent moments, softly wrapped,
In winter's arms, we're gently trapped.
The world outside, a canvas white,
Beneath the stars, our hearts alight.

Whispers linger, join the dance,
In merriment, we take a chance.
With every glance, the magic swirls,
In winter's joy, our spirit twirls.

Laughter echoes, crisp and clear,
Every giggle brings us near.
Underneath the moon's soft glow,
In the quiet, love will grow.

Beneath the blanket of pure white,
We find our heartbeats, pure delight.
With every breath, a new refrain,
In winter's song, we break the chain.

Winterscape of Forgotten Hopes

In a winterscape, all is bright,
Sparkling dreams take joyful flight.
The hearth is warm, the candles glow,
In the stillness, love will flow.

Snowy branches, crisp and clear,
In every corner, we find cheer.
With every toast and joyful song,
We gather close, where we belong.

Forgotten hopes now come alive,
In this magic, we all thrive.
Through flurries wild, our hearts align,
In festive cheer, our souls entwine.

So gather 'round, in love's embrace,
With every smile, we find our place.
In winterscape, our spirits soar,
Together we'll forever adore.

Canvas of White

Snowflakes dance in the glow,
Children laugh, hearts aglow.
Trees in whispers, they sway,
Winter's magic leads the way.

Carols sung, joy in the air,
Frosty breath, a moment rare.
Hot cocoa warms the weary soul,
Together we create our whole.

Portrait of Yearning

Stars alight on a velvet sky,
Dreams take wing, as wishes fly.
In the hush, the world holds tight,
Hope whispers soft through the night.

Love ignites in the silent chill,
Every heartbeat, a spark to thrill.
Together, we paint our night bright,
In the canvas of frosty light.

Heartbeats Lost in the Snowfall

Silent snowfalls blanket the ground,
Lost in wonder, joy is found.
Footprints mark the playful spree,
In this wonderland, we are free.

Laughter dances in frosty air,
Moments paused, without a care.
Heartbeats echo, a rhythmic play,
In the snowfall, we lose our way.

The Quietude of Frosted Dreams

Whispers of snow in the night,
Breath of winter, pure delight.
Underneath a blanket white,
Frosty dreams take gentle flight.

Stars twinkle like memories near,
Carrying laughter, love, and cheer.
In the quiet, hearts entwine,
Frosted dreams like rarest wine.

A Labyrinth of Frozen Thoughts

In the maze of falling snow,
Thoughts drift softly, ebb and flow.
Each flake tells a tale anew,
Of hopes and dreams that we pursue.

Paths intertwine, and we explore,
Leading to cozy, warm décor.
In this labyrinth, hearts get lost,
Finding warmth, no matter the frost.

Crystal Dreams on Silent Nights

Stars twinkle bright in the sky,
Laughter echoes as we pass by.
Candles flicker, warm the cold,
Stories of joy lovingly told.

Snowflakes fall, a soft embrace,
Children play, with smiles on their face.
Hot cocoa steams in gentle hands,
Magic whispers across the lands.

Twinkling lights hang on each tree,
Creating a world of harmony.
Crystal dreams spark to ignite,
Hearts are light on this festive night.

The Stillness Within the Storm

Amidst the chaos, peace can bloom,
Songs of joy dispel the gloom.
Colors dance in swirling light,
A festive spirit takes its flight.

Beneath the noise, a warmth we find,
Gathered close, all heart aligned.
Laughter rings through winter's air,
In this moment, no trace of care.

Snowflakes swirl, a graceful line,
Embracing us, our hearts entwined.
Together we stand, brave and bold,
In the stillness, stories unfold.

Chilling Embrace of the Unknown

Whispers float where shadows play,
Mysterious winds sweep dreams away.
Candles glow with a flickering light,
Filling hearts with pure delight.

Nights unfold with secrets to share,
In the chill, we breathe fresh air.
Laughter bursts, transcending fright,
United, we dance through the night.

Embrace the unknown, let it be sweet,
With every step, a new heartbeat.
Twisting paths, wild and free,
In this festive realm, we're meant to be.

Shadows Danced on Frosted Ground

Beneath the moon, where shadows play,
Frosted whispers greet the day.
Footprints left in sparkling snow,
A festive chill in the air aglow.

Fires crackle, bright and bold,
Tales of wonder warmly told.
Hands held tight, a circle we weave,
In this moment, we truly believe.

Stars above twinkle, joy impart,
Binding us with a festive heart.
Dancing shadows, wild and free,
In the night, we're meant to be.

A Heart Entombed in Ice

In twilight's embrace, the silence sings,
A heart encased in winter's rings.
The stars above, like crystals bright,
Illuminate the long, cold night.

Laughter echoes through the trees,
A joyful sound, carried by the breeze.
With every breath, the magic spins,
As warmth ignites where the chill begins.

Fires crackle, dance, and sway,
Uniting souls in festive play.
From icy grips, the heart takes flight,
In festive cheer, it claims the night.

Frost Flowers Blooming Quietly

Beneath the snow, soft petals hide,
Nature's beauty, wrapped with pride.
In gentle folds, their colors gleam,
Winter's artistry, a waking dream.

Through frosty air, the laughter floats,
In whispered tunes, the spirit gloats.
Every flake, a spark of grace,
Filling hearts in this sacred space.

The world adorned in shining white,
Under the gaze of the moon's light.
In every corner, joy is found,
As love and warmth sweep all around.

Echoes of the Winter Wind

The winter wind, it calls our name,
In every gust, it fans the flame.
With joyful hearts, we gather near,
To share old tales, to spread the cheer.

Snowflakes fall like soft confetti,
Dancing lightly, ever ready.
With laughter bright and voices bold,
We share the warmth against the cold.

In every note, in every sound,
The festive spirit wraps around.
As echoes rise, the night awakes,
With joyous songs the heart partakes.

Silence in a Shroud of White

In quiet hours, the snow descends,
A shroud of calm, where silence blends.
The world transformed, pure and bright,
Wrapped in peace, a wondrous sight.

The laughter stirs the still, deep night,
As friends unite in warm delight.
In every corner, joy a sign,
The shimmer of the stars align.

Beneath the moon's embrace so light,
We gather close, hearts held tight.
In shouts of glee, we cast aside,
The festive warmth that swells with pride.

Chilled Whispers of Winter

Gentle snowflakes drift and dance,
A joyful tune, a sweet romance.
Laughter bubbles, warm and bright,
In the glow of winter's light.

Cocoa steaming, hearts aglow,
Around the fire, friendships grow.
Merry songs on lips do play,
In this festive winter's day.

Frostbitten Dreams

Stars twinkle in the crisp, clear night,
Frosted branches sparkle bright.
Children's giggles fill the air,
Snowball fights without a care.

Lights twirl on every street,
Joyful hearts skip to the beat.
Magic whispers in the breeze,
Winter's wonder, hearts to seize.

Silent Identities in White

Blankets soft, a planet dressed,
Whispers soft in winter's nest.
Chilled embraces, cozy and warm,
In every flake, a new charm.

Shadows dance in moonlight's glow,
Silent stories wrapped in snow.
Each breath visible, crisp and clear,
Radiant joy, the time of year.

Bound by Frost's Embrace

Underneath a silver sky,
Snowflakes twirl, and children sigh.
In this frosty, joyous dance,
Take a moment, lose your glance.

Candles flicker in the dark,
Holding close that warming spark.
With each laugh and hug we share,
Winter's magic fills the air.

Serenity in a Shimmering Land

In a land where the stars play,
The moon kisses the gentle sway,
Whispers of joy fill the night,
A tapestry woven with light.

Glittering snow blankets the ground,
Each flake a jewel, softly found,
Laughter echoes in the air,
An enchantment beyond compare.

Children twirl with such delight,
Chasing shadows with purest might,
Fires crackle, warmth all around,
In this haven, love knows no bounds.

As dawn breaks with colors bright,
The world awakens, pure and right,
Serenity, a gentle hand,
Holding dreams in a shimmering land.

A Tapestry of White and Woe

Beneath the frost, the ground is still,
Silence wrapped in a winter chill,
Yet hearts beat loud against the freeze,
A tapestry woven with unease.

Frosted trees stand tall and bare,
Echoes of laughter fill the air,
Yet shadows lurk in the soft glow,
A reminder of paths filled with woe.

Candles flicker, casting light,
Through the darkness, a hopeful sight,
Yet memories linger, bittersweet,
In this dance where joy may retreat.

Yet hope ignites in every hue,
A promise of warmth breaking through,
A tapestry of white and woe,
Woven tight in life's gentle flow.

The Dance of Snowflakes and Dreams

Snowflakes twirl like whispered dreams,
Dancing softly through moonlight beams,
Each one unique, a story unfolds,
In the chill, a magic behold.

Laughter drifts on a frosted breeze,
Spirits soar with joyful ease,
As children chase the flurries down,
In their hearts, they wear a crown.

Warm mugs hug chilly hands,
As stories sway like shifting sands,
Candles flicker, glow so bright,
Enveloping the world in light.

In the hush, dreams take their flight,
Snowflakes dance in the starry night,
A festivity stitched in time,
Where every heart can gently rhyme.

A Heart Chilled by Time

In the moment, time seems still,
Candles burn on windowsills,
Yet the clock ticks, a subtle chime,
Echoing truths of a heart chilled by time.

Snow blankets all with tender care,
A hush surrounds the frosty air,
Memories dance with shadows past,
Whispers of joy that forever last.

Through drifts of white, we walk in peace,
Finding warmth, a sweet release,
In gatherings, laughter fills the room,
A heart's chill fades in the bloom.

Yet time, it races, never slow,
In every moment, let love grow,
For even hearts chilled can refine,
In the warmth of a festive design.

Echoes Caught in the Snow

Laughter dances upon the breeze,
Joyful voices, a symphony of glee.
Colorful lights twinkle in the night,
Celebration sparkles, oh what a sight.

Children play in soft, drifting flakes,
Building memories that the heart makes.
Winter's embrace, cozy and bright,
Echoes of cheer fill the starry night.

The warmth of cocoa in gloved hands,
Fires crackle, as happiness expands.
Songs of the season, sweetly they flow,
In the magic of winter, love starts to grow.

Let the snowflakes twirl down around,
In this joyful season, peace is found.
With each step, let the laughter increase,
In the echoes caught, we find our peace.

Dreaming Beneath Frosted Skies

Under blankets of white, dreams take flight,
Stars twinkle softly like jewels at night.
The world is hushed, wrapped in a glow,
Hearts beat slowly, letting love flow.

Candles flicker, casting warm light,
Whispers of wishes drift through the night.
Frosted windows frame the scene,
A portrait of warmth, tranquil and serene.

Gathered together, we share our tales,
Of magic and wonder, whispers on gales.
The chill in the air, sweetened with cheer,
In our hearts, the festive spirit draws near.

As snowflakes swirl, we raise a glass,
To the moments we cherish as seasons pass.
Dreaming beneath the frosted skies,
In this wondrous season, our spirits rise.

The Frozen Path of Forgotten Days

Footprints marked in a blanket of snow,
Memories linger, though time moves slow.
Laughter echoes down the frozen path,
Binding us closer, preventing the wrath.

Carols sung with joy, fill the air,
Hearts entwined, in love and care.
The scent of pine, fresh and divine,
Brings back whispers of days intertwine.

Crisp winter nights, with stars shining bright,
We gather around, sharing delight.
The warmth of old stories, passed down with pride,
In the frozen embrace, we stand side by side.

Though days may fade, and seasons may change,
The love of the past, it will never estrange.
So let us walk on this path anew,
In the spirit of joy, with hearts ever true.

Chill of the Velvet Night

As stars twinkle on the velvet expanse,
The chill in the air invites us to dance.
With lights all aglow, our spirits ignite,
In the magic of winter, hearts feel so light.

Snowflakes whisper secrets they share,
In the quiet of night, a moment so rare.
Joyous laughter erupts in the cold,
As stories of warmth and friendship unfold.

Together we gather, beneath frosty trees,
Sipping on cocoa, feeling the breeze.
The chill wraps around, yet warms every soul,
In the heart of the night, together we're whole.

So let the chill of the velvet night reign,
With love as our guide, we will not refrain.
In festive delight, we find peace and cheer,
The joy of the season, forever held dear.

The Ghosts of Winter's Embrace

In whispers light, the shadows dance,
They twirl and sway, a silent trance.
Through frosty nights, the stars alight,
The ghosts of winter take their flight.

A blanket white on earth so still,
Each flake a dream, a gentle thrill.
With laughter bright, the children play,
In winter's grip, they find their way.

The chilly breath, a crisp delight,
Inviting warmth could feel just right.
As candles glow in homes aglow,
The festive cheer begins to flow.

So hold fast tight to joy's embrace,
In winter's hold, our hearts find grace.
With every jest and every song,
The ghosts of winter help us long.

A Solitary Journey through the Snow

Alone I walk on paths of white,
The world aglow in silver light.
Each crunch beneath, a melody,
A symphony of peace with me.

The trees stand tall with arms outspread,
In frosty coats, their branches wed.
A gentle breeze, it stirs the night,
Whispers of dreams, so soft, so right.

With every step, I find my pace,
The solitude, a warm embrace.
The stars above, my guiding spark,
Illuminate this silent park.

Through winter's hush, my spirit sings,
While Christmas joy around me clings.
A solitary path I tread,
And in my heart, the warmth is spread.

Glassy Images of a Frigid Heart

Reflections glint on icy streams,
Where winter's chill erases dreams.
A heart encased in fragile glass,
Each moment fleeting, quick to pass.

Yet in the stillness, hope remains,
A spark of joy that softly gains.
With every shard, a tale retold,
In patterns bright, and colors bold.

Around the fire, we gather near,
To share the warmth, to quell the fear.
The laughter rings, a vibrant sound,
In frosty air, our hearts are found.

So let us raise our cups in cheer,
For every friend who lingers here.
Though icy hearts may feel so stark,
Together we can light the dark.

Candor in the Winter's Grip

The air is crisp, the night is clear,
With laughter bright, we spread good cheer.
In every home, a hearth aglow,
As winter's grip begins to show.

Families gather, stories unfold,
In cozy rooms, the warmth we hold.
With open hearts, our spirits bloom,
While winter winds paint every room.

The table set with joy and grace,
The festive feast in every space.
Beneath the twinkle of the lights,
On winter's eve, our love ignites.

So let us toast to days like these,
With frost outside and hearts at ease.
In winter's hold, the warmth we find,
A candor shared, forever kind.

A Soul Enshrined in Frost

Amidst the twinkling winter's grace,
Where laughter dances, time's embrace,
The world adorned in fields of white,
A celebration, pure delight.

Fireworks crackle in the night,
With joyful hearts, we gather tight,
Warmth of friends, stories unfold,
In frosty air, our dreams are bold.

Songs of cheer fill every space,
As voices blend in merry chase,
With glistening stars, we raise our cheer,
In this enchanted time of year.

As whispers weave through snowy skies,
We find the magic that never dies,
A soul enshrined, in frost it gleams,
In every heart, the warmth of dreams.

Snowy Boundaries of the Heart

The snowflakes fall, a soft ballet,
Each flurry twirls in bright display,
Beneath the sky, both wide and clear,
The boundaries fade, love draws us near.

Glimmering lights on every tree,
Their radiance sings of jubilee,
In crisp air, joy takes its flight,
Hearts entwined, our spirits bright.

Around the hearth, we share our tales,
With laughter's echo, warmth prevails,
As snow blankets the world outside,
In cozy corners, we abide.

Fireside glow, a soothing balm,
In festive cheer, we find our calm,
Snowy boundaries, no longer apart,
In every flake, a beating heart.

The Whispering Pines in a Slumbering Land

In winter's hush, the pines do sway,
As whispers echo, night and day,
They speak of joy, of seasons' cheer,
In slumbering lands so calm and clear.

Beneath a quilt of silvered white,
The world is wrapped, a pure delight,
We wander through this dreamlike place,
Finding warmth in love's embrace.

With every step, the crunch of snow,
A melody of warmth does flow,
Together, we embrace the night,
In the pines, our hearts take flight.

Each sigh of wind, a gentle song,
In festive bliss, we all belong,
The whispering pines hold secrets dear,
As laughter dances through the year.

Shards of Ice in a Still Breath

In the stillness, ice begins to gleam,
With shards of light like diamonds' dream,
Reflecting hope in winter's glow,
A festive spirit, soft and slow.

The world adorned in frosty lace,
We gather round, a warm embrace,
With every cheer, our voices rise,
In the calm, love never dies.

Candles flicker with gentle grace,
Drawing shadows on each face,
In icy air, our laughter rings,
As joy unfolds, our spirit sings.

Holding hands beneath the stars,
We cherish dreams, we break down bars,
Shards of ice, in stillness found,
In festive hearts, our love abounds.

The Crystal Prism of Reminiscence

In halls adorned with lights aglow,
Reflections dance, a vibrant show.
Laughter echoes, sweet and clear,
As memories join us, drawing near.

With every flicker, stories play,
Of moments cherished, come what may.
Each sparkling hue, a tale retold,
In crystal prisms, memories unfold.

We raise our glasses, toast the night,
To friendships forged, in joy's pure light.
The air is filled with music's charm,
In unity, we feel the warm.

So gather close, let spirits soar,
In this embrace, we seek for more.
Together bound, we'll share our dreams,
In festive glow, life's magic gleams.

Solitude Beneath the Snowfall

Beneath the hush of falling snow,
A gentle silence starts to grow.
Wrapped in white, the world transforms,
In solitude, a peace abounds.

Each flake that lands, a whispered cheer,
A blanket soft, that draws us near.
Footprints trace the path we roam,
In winter's grip, we find our home.

The stars above, a twinkling dance,
Inviting hearts to take a chance.
In frosty air, our breath like smoke,
We share our dreams, with every joke.

Though quiet reigns, the joy runs deep,
In snowy realms, our hearts will leap.
Together here, we weave our tales,
In solitude, our spirit sails.

A Heart Adrift in Frozen Dreams

In frozen landscapes, hearts will glide,
On icy paths where hopes reside.
We dance on shards of crystal light,
As dreams take flight in heart's delight.

Each breath is drawn in winter's chill,
Yet warmth arises, soft and still.
With every turn, excitement grows,
As winds of fortune gently blow.

The stars above, like lanterns shine,
Celestial whispers, voices entwined.
In this embrace of night divine,
Our frozen dreams, they brightly shine.

So let us wander, hand in hand,
In this enchanted, frosty land.
A heart adrift, in joy we gleam,
In twilight's glow, we chase our dream.

Threads of Ice weaving Memories

In winter's weave, the stories flow,
Threads of ice, they intertwine slow.
Wrapped in white, the past unfolds,
As secrets shared, like jewels, hold.

Each sparkling strand, a memory made,
In swirling winds, our laughter played.
With every stitch, the warmth we find,
A tapestry of heart and mind.

Through frosted panes, the world we see,
Reflecting back, sweet harmony.
In this embrace of icy grace,
We lose ourselves in time and space.

So gather close, and hold on tight,
To threads we weave in joyous light.
In winter's charm, our spirits blend,
In memories stitched, love has no end.

Enchanted by the Frost's Serenity

In the glow of winter nights,
Laughter dances on the breeze.
Snowflakes waltz in pure delight,
Whispering secrets through the trees.

Frost adorns each window pane,
A crystal world, a wondrous spell.
Friends gather round, no hint of pain,
Sharing stories they know so well.

Candles flicker, warm and bright,
Hearts embrace the chill outside.
Magic weaves through the starlit night,
Together, we bask in joy and pride.

With every cheer and toasty cup,
We sip on dreams of days to come.
In this moment, we lift our hearts up,
To frosty joys, we all succumb.

Lament of the Snowbound Wanderer

Underneath the heavy sky,
I tread soft on blanket white.
Each flake whispers a goodbye,
Loneliness grips the fading light.

Footsteps echo, though I'm one,
Lost in realms of dream and frost.
The warmth of home feels far from done,
In this silence, I feel the cost.

Yet still the stars begin to glow,
Their twinkle brings the promise near.
I find hope in the falling snow,
A reminder that spring will clear.

I raise my voice into the chill,
A festive song to face the night.
For even bound, my heart can thrill,
In frost, I find my own delight.

A Canvas Painted in Soft Whiteness

Upon a field of velvet white,
Nature sprawls in wild embrace.
Each flake brings peace with gentle flight,
A serene hush, a snowy grace.

Children laugh, their joy untamed,
Building dreams in hills of snow.
Carrots, scarves, in art unframed,
Winter's wonders start to grow.

Branches draped in icy gems,
Glittering in the soft-lit glow.
Magic dances, nature hems,
A tapestry of purest flow.

With every breathe, the world feels bright,
And hearts are light, as snowflakes play.
In this moment, pure delight,
A canvas frames a winter's day.

Crystalline Reflections of Obscured Love

In the stillness, hearts collide,
Mirrored by the frosty glass.
Secrets linger, yet abide,
In the shadows, memories pass.

Snowflakes fall like whispered dreams,
Each one holds our hidden sighs.
Crystalline truth, the silence gleams,
Soft illumination in the skies.

The night enfolds our secrets tight,
Underneath the moon's soft gaze.
In this chill, our hearts take flight,
Dancing through the winter's haze.

So here we stand, with love oblique,
In frost, our laughter soon will bloom.
Crystalline, our words may peek,
In winter's grasp, we find our room.

The Icy Gaze of a Winter's Night

Stars twinkle like diamonds bright,
In the frost of a winter's night.
Snowflakes dance with gentle grace,
Blanketing the world in a lace.

Fires crackle with stories old,
Warmth inside while outside cold.
Laughter rings, the air so light,
Joy surrounds us, pure delight.

Children's faces glow with cheer,
As carols sung bring everyone near.
With cocoa in hand, hearts ignite,
Under the Icy Gaze of night.

Every moment, a treasure rare,
Shared together, a bond to bear.
In this season, spirits take flight,
Embracing the Icy Gaze of night.

Beneath the White Silence

Beneath a blanket so soft and white,
Nature sleeps, all is quiet tonight.
Footsteps muffled, a gentle scene,
Wrapped in peace, everything serene.

Hushed whispers of the wind so sweet,
Dance through branches, a rhythmic beat.
Frost-kissed air, so pure and bright,
Embraces us, hearts feel light.

Families gather, love surrounds,
Echoes of laughter, joy abounds.
Together we share this special night,
Beneath the White Silence, so right.

With every breath, the magic flows,
In this moment, happiness glows.
Nights like this, we hold so tight,
Beneath the stars and soft moonlight.

Heartbeats in a Snowy Haze

Amidst the snowfall, hearts collide,
In the frosty air, joy can't hide.
With every laugh, with every cheer,
The warmth of love draws us near.

Snowballs flying, a playful sight,
Chasing shadows in pure delight.
Candles flicker, casting a glow,
Heartbeats quicken as embers flow.

Gathered close, we share our dreams,
Under twinkling, starry beams.
Snowy wonder wraps us tight,
In this haze, everything feels right.

With every heartbeat, a promise made,
In this winter magic, fears will fade.
Together we shine, a radiant blaze,
Heartbeats dance in a snowy haze.

Lullabies of the Winter Moon

The winter moon casts silver light,
Whispering dreams to the silent night.
Branches sway with graceful ease,
Carrying secrets on the chilly breeze.

Softly falling, the snowflakes play,
A lullaby for the end of day.
Wrapped in warmth, we close our eyes,
Listening close to the moonlit sighs.

Stories told 'neath the blanket of stars,
Of distant lands, and love that's ours.
With every twinkle, our hopes bloom,
Swaying gently to the winter's tune.

In this peace, the world feels small,
As the winter moon watches over all.
Together we dream, held tight in this room,
Cradled softly by lullabies of the winter moon.

The Cold Cradle of Reflection

In the twilight, candles glow bright,
Families gather, hearts feel light.
Laughter dances on winter's breeze,
As joy whispers through frosted trees.

Snowflakes settle, a tapestry spun,
Each one's a story, a time of fun.
Memories sparkle in the chilled air,
Warmth of love is everywhere.

Chocolates shared, stories unfold,
Around the fire, the magic is bold.
Hope and dreams twinkle like stars,
In the cold cradle, forget your scars.

With every toast, the night lifts high,
Under a blanket of the moonlit sky.
In this embrace, we find our place,
The cold cradle, a warm, gentle space.

Frost-kissed Memories

Frost on windows, a delicate art,
Whispers of winter, a fresh start.
Glittering paths of white, pure delight,
Sending us dreaming into the night.

Children play, their laughter rings,
Bundled in scarves, with joy it springs.
In this wonderland, spirits soar,
Frost-kissed memories, forevermore.

The warmth of cocoa in every hand,
Sipping slowly, together we stand.
Sharing stories wrapped in cheer,
The essence of love, always near.

With each glance, connections grow,
In this season where kindness flows.
Frost-kissed moments, soft and sweet,
In this festive joy, our hearts repeat.

A Soul Wrapped in Frost

Wrapped in warmth, through chill we glide,
Hearts united, side by side.
Each breath forms clouds in the night air,
A soul wrapped in frost, light as a prayer.

Music echoes from door to door,
Carols sung, spirits soar.
Under the stars, we dance and spin,
In this embrace, true joy begins.

Candles flicker with a golden hue,
Casting shadows, the night feels new.
Every smile a beacon, bright and bold,
A tale of warmth in the winter's fold.

Gathered close, stories to share,
A soul wrapped in frost, love fills the air.
Together we cherish the moments we find,
In the festive magic, our hearts intertwined.

Glistening Chains of Winter's Grasp

Glistening chains of winter's hold,
Sparkling jewels in the night, untold.
Each branch draped in a coat of white,
A vision of wonder, pure delight.

As lanterns flicker, shadows dance,
In the charm of night, we find our chance.
Snowflakes twirl to a silent tune,
With every breath, we greet the moon.

The warmth of laughter fuels the cold,
Together in stories, hearts unfold.
Pine-scented dreams twine with the frost,
In this festive glow, nothing is lost.

Chains of glimmer wrap us tight,
Filling our souls with sheer delight.
Winter's grasp, a delicate art,
In this season, we weave our heart.

The Winter's Grasp on the Soul

Winter whispers soft and low,
Frosted breath in moonlit glow.
Laughter dances in the air,
Joyful hearts beyond compare.

Snowflakes twirl, a merry chase,
Underneath the starry grace.
Fires crackle, warmth ignites,
Sharing stories, cozy nights.

Glistening fields in silver sheen,
Nature dons her crystal scene.
Hand in hand, we stroll along,
In this bliss, we all belong.

Beneath the trees adorned in white,
We find magic, pure delight.
As winter's grasp holds tight and close,
In love, our hearts forever boast.

The Snowflakes' Gentle Lament

Snowflakes fall like whispered dreams,
Filling paths with silver gleams.
Each one tells a tale untold,
Of warmth and cheer in winter's fold.

Gently landing, soft and light,
Transforming scenes from day to night.
Laughter echoes, children play,
Chasing snowflakes on the way.

Hot cocoa flows, sweet aromas rise,
As family gathers, love never dies.
Together we share these moments rare,
In the warmth of hearts that truly care.

While the world outside may freeze,
Inside, hearts dance with joyous ease.
For in every flake that falls,
A reminder of love's sweet calls.

A Chill Underneath the Stars

Underneath a sky so bright,
Stars like diamonds sprinkle light.
The chilly breeze begins to play,
Whispers of night usher the day.

Candles flicker, shadows dance,
Inviting us to take a chance.
With every step, the snowflakes sigh,
As laughter weaves through the sky.

The air is crisp, our spirits high,
Beneath this vast and twinkling sky.
We gather close, united near,
In moments captured, crystal clear.

With hearts aglow, we find our cheer,
In the magic of this time of year.
For underneath the starry dome,
We feel in winter, very much at home.

The Serenity of a Frozen Heart

In the hush of winter's eve,
Silent moments softly weave.
A frozen heart can start to thaw,
In the midst of nature's awe.

Blankets white on slumbering ground,
Peaceful whispers all around.
Each snowflake's fall, a gentle kiss,
In every touch, we find our bliss.

Families gather, voices blend,
In warmth and love, our hearts transcend.
As laughter sparkles in the air,
We find the joy that we all share.

In winter's chill, our spirits rise,
Finding solace in the skies.
For in each snow, a promise gleams,
Of love's embrace and cherished dreams.

Frozen Echoes of Solitude

In the quiet night, stars gleam bright,
Whispers of laughter, pure delight.
Snowflakes dance in the frosty air,
Echoes of joy, everywhere.

Candles flicker, shadows play,
Families gather, night turns to day.
Warmth in hearts, the cold can't steal,
Festivities wrapped in the winter's reel.

Songs of cheer rise through the cold,
Stories of love are quietly told.
With every heartbeat, spirits soar,
In the frozen night, we ask for more.

Beneath the moon's soft, silver glow,
The world in white, a stunning show.
In this beauty, sadness fades,
Frozen echoes, joy cascades.

Winter's Veil Over Heartstrings

Snowy whispers on the breeze,
Glistening branches sway with ease.
Softly falls the shimmering white,
Wrapping the world in pure delight.

Joyful laughter fills the air,
Though chilly winds might seem unfair.
Hearts aglow with festive cheer,
Winter's veil draws loved ones near.

In cozy nooks, stories shared,
Each moment cherished, hearts are bared.
Under twinkling lights we sing,
Embracing what the season brings.

With love and laughter, spirits rise,
In winter's arms, we close our eyes.
The warmth prevails, the cold's embrace,
Festive magic in every space.

Shattered Silence of the Snowfall

Silent nights where shadows play,
Snowflakes drift, then fade away.
Hearts awaken, spirits gleam,
In this quiet, we dare to dream.

Fires crackle, warmth ignites,
Laughter echoes through the nights.
Together we chase the winter's chill,
In cozy moments, time stands still.

Mittens clasped, we spin and twirl,
In a world as white as pearl.
Every flake, a wish anew,
In the silence, joy breaks through.

Through the snowfall, memories flow,
A festive spirit all aglow.
In the stillness, our hearts can see,
Magic found in symmetry.

Embracing the Icy Emptiness

Crisp air bites, yet hearts ignite,
Frosted landscapes, pure and bright.
Candles burn with a golden hue,
Embracing moments, old and new.

Hushed whispers linger in the night,
Wrapped in warmth, we feel the light.
Smiles exchanged, we share a glance,
In winter's grip, we find our dance.

Blankets piled, stories unfold,
In icy emptiness, love is bold.
Family warmth dispels the cold,
In festive echoes, we are consoled.

Together we stand, hand in hand,
Facing the chill, as we planned.
In the emptiness, we hear the song,
That whispers to us, we all belong.

Muffled Cries Beneath the Snow

In hushed tones, whispers glide,
Snowflakes dance, a gentle ride.
Laughter hidden, soft and bright,
Nature's blanket, pure delight.

Children play in snowy fields,
Joyful secrets, warmth it yields.
Footsteps trace a frosty path,
Echoes of the season's laugh.

Carols rise with each fresh gust,
Sparkling lights in evening's hush.
Underneath the swirling flurry,
Hearts unite in happy hurry.

The world is wrapped in purest white,
A festive glow, a twinkling light.
Muffled cries bring cheer anew,
Winter's canvas, bright and true.

The Frosted Mirror of My Mind

Reflections dance like shimmering glass,
Whispers of joy as moments pass.
Memories twirl in frosty air,
Radiant smiles beyond compare.

Glints of laughter break the cold,
Tales of wonder quietly told.
In this mirror, dreams take flight,
Frosted visions, pure delight.

Sparkling thoughts weave through the night,
Guided by the stars' soft light.
A festive spirit, wild and free,
Captured in this mystery.

Time stands still on winter's breath,
Life's embrace, a dance with death.
Yet, in the chill, warmth finds its way,
Rekindling joy for a brighter day.

Veils of Winter's Quietude

Beneath the silent, starry skies,
Whispers float where hope still lies.
Veils of white, a tranquil scene,
Blanket dreams of what has been.

Frosty branches softly sway,
Hushed the night where children play.
Filled with love, the air is sweet,
Festive moments, hearts repeat.

Glistening lights on every street,
Joyful echoes in winter's heat.
Carved in ice, the laughter flows,
In winter's care, our spirit grows.

Cups raised high in joyful cheer,
Togetherness that draws us near.
In winter's arms, a cozy hold,
Veils of magic, bright and bold.

Ember's Warmth in Cold Embrace

Crackling fires, a glowing sight,
Embers dance in the cozy night.
Sipping cider, laughter sings,
Together, warmth this evening brings.

Blankets piled in gentle heaps,
Chasing shadows, the spirit leaps.
Outside the frost, inside the glow,
Ember's warmth, a festive flow.

Stories shared as time slips by,
Dreams ignite like sparks on high.
Hearts aglow with the season's grace,
In cold embrace, we find our place.

Wishing wells and holiday cheer,
Each ember whispers, love is near.
In the stillness of the night,
Together, we make everything right.

The Silence of a Snowy Evening

Snowflakes dance like stars, oh so bright,
Whispers of winter, pure delight.
Blankets of white on the sleeping ground,
In this embrace, peace can be found.

Laughter of children, warm and near,
Frosty breaths echo, full of cheer.
Huddled around fires, tales we share,
In the snowy silence, love fills the air.

Frozen Reveries of the Heart

Icicles glisten, a crystal display,
Hearts beat softly as night turns to day.
Dreams wrapped in warmth, snug and tight,
In frozen reveries, we take flight.

Stars twinkle brightly, a celestial glow,
Hopes intertwined like branches that grow.
Each moment cherished, a memory made,
In winter's embrace, our fears start to fade.

In the Grip of Winter's Tenderness

Soft winds whisper through the frosted trees,
Carrying laughter on the chilly breeze.
Bundled up warm in colors so bold,
Stories unfold, with each breath we hold.

Warm cocoa sipped by fireside glow,
Hearts aglow as the soft embers flow.
In winter's tender grip, joy ignites,
Painting the world in magical sights.

The Winter's Song of a Lonely Spirit

Lonely spirits roam the night,
Singing softly in pale moonlight.
Snow blankets whispers, a soft refrain,
In this quiet, joy mingles with pain.

Yet even in silence, hope does gleam,
Creating warmth from the cold, a dream.
Through winter's song, we find our way,
Where love's light shines, dispelling dismay.

Chasing Light Through Blizzards

In swirling snow, we dance and spin,
With laughter bright, igniting kin.
A glow of warmth in winter's chill,
We chase the light, our hearts fulfill.

The frosty air bursts with delight,
As snowflakes twirl, pure and white.
We sing of joy, a merry tune,
While stars above begin to swoon.

Together we gather, hand in hand,
Amidst the drifts, we make our stand.
With every breath, the world feels bright,
In blizzards fierce, we chase the light.

So let us twirl where shadows play,
And dance till dawn on winter's day.
With hearts aglow and spirits high,
We'll chase the light 'neath twilight sky.

Whispers of a Frosted Heart

In twilight's hush, the whispers speak,
Of frosted dreams and love we seek.
A gentle breeze through boughs will sway,
In winter's grasp, we'll find our way.

Each glimmering flake, a secret told,
Of warmth and hope in the bitter cold.
Through icy paths, our hearts take flight,
In whispered vows, we'll love the night.

The world transformed, a crystalline scene,
In frosted silence, we reign supreme.
With every pulse, a soft embrace,
As winter's song fills empty space.

So come with me, let's dance and glide,
With frost our veil, and joy our guide.
In snowy realms where magic starts,
We'll share our dreams, our frosted hearts.

Frozen Echoes of Solitude

In silent woods where shadows hide,
Echoes linger, soft and wide.
Through silver trees, the whispers roam,
In solitude, we find our home.

The crunch of snow beneath our feet,
In frozen air, the stillness sweet.
Each breath a cloud in crystal light,
We wander far, alone, yet bright.

With every step, the world stands still,
In nature's arms, we find the thrill.
A tapestry of white and blue,
In frozen dreams, we start anew.

So let the echoes softly call,
In solitude, we'll rise and fall.
Through winter's song, a peaceful thread,
In frozen echoes, hearts are fed.

Beneath the Winter Veil

Beneath the snow, the world sleeps tight,
Embraced in dreams of purest white.
A hush envelops, calm and deep,
While quiet nights gently creep.

The gentle glow of moonlit skies,
Where every star a promise lies.
With frosty breath, we share the night,
As winter's charm ignites our light.

Each flake that falls, a whispered prayer,
In hidden realms, we wander there.
With every step, a journey starts,
Beneath the veil, we bind our hearts.

So let us dream in winter's grace,
With cozy fires and a warm embrace.
In this enchanted, snowy tale,
Together we'll thrive beneath the veil.